essent

Help Your 3–5 Year Old Learn Through Rhymes, Riddles and Songs

Help Your
3–5 Year Old Learn
Through Rhymes,
Riddles and Songs

Ken Adams

PARENTS' ESSENTIALS

Published in 2000 by
How To Books Ltd, 3 Newtec Place,
Magdalen Road, Oxford OX4 1RE, United Kingdom
Tel: (01865) 793806   Fax: (01865) 248780
email: info@howtobooks.co.uk
www.howtobooks.co.uk

British Library Cataloguing in Publication Data.
A catalogue record for this book is available from
the British Library.

Cover design by Shireen Nathoo Design
Produced for How To Books by Deer Park Productions
Typeset by PDQ Typesetting, Newcastle-under-Lyme, Staffordshire
Printed and bound by Hillman Printers, Frome, Somerset

ESSENTIALS *is an imprint of*
How To Books

Contents

Preface

Increasingly nowadays, parents are becoming involved with their child's education. This includes helping their pre-school child as well as the child who is already at school. There is a perception that encouragement at home can improve a child's chances in later work and exams. Success, even in simple learning, can breed confidence, which quite often translates into confidence in the classroom.

Rhymes, riddles and songs have involved parents and children for as long as most of us can remember. Parents often know the rhymes extremely well, and can also remember the tunes associated with them. In addition, rhymes can be learnt from a very young age. Finger rhymes are often taught to babies and young toddlers. Such a tradition of enjoyment of play, teaches many aspects of early learning. The purpose of this book is to point out where a small emphasis on certain aspects of rhymes, riddles and songs can result in considerable learning benefits for the very young child.

There is no suggestion of interfering with play and natural enjoyment, but rather of being aware of how your child's potential can be realised through already established and enjoyed activities.

Ken Adams

1 Learning with Rhymes

Rhymes have been used for centuries by parents to communicate with their young children through rhythm and actions. A side development of this is the increase of vocabulary, because the use of actions and the rhyme itself aids visualisation. Communication is non-demanding, so learning is relaxed and easy. Concrete words like 'book', 'boy', 'man', tree' and so on, are easily learnt, but so are action words like 'eat', drink', 'run', 'sleep'. There are also good counting rhymes that can be sung to your child as they walk up the stairs at bedtime, or walk along the road counting steps. Listening to rhymes and joining in with the actions can teach many rudimentary skills to a pre-school child, and such activities bring great enjoyment to the learner – nursery rhymes and associated tunes are often remembered throughout one's whole life.

COMMUNICATION STIMULATES INTEREST

The pre-school years form an extremely important time for building a foundation of knowledge on which further learning can be built. This later learning is often abstract – for example, using the written word and numbers – and without a wide basis and good depth of understanding of the real world, schoolwork can founder.

This importance of early learning makes it essential that you communicate effectively with your child, particularly in an enjoyable way, so that word knowledge is extended, and very simple mathematical ideas (numbers, shape) become part of their everyday thinking. Making rhymes, riddles and action songs appropriate to the age of your child is one of the best ways to build this early thinking, particularly if it stimulates conversation and other forms of communication with you, the parent. In the first place, your child will be pleased that you are interested in what they are doing and thinking. There are times, of course, when children need to play by themselves – to relive what they see in real life, and to try to test the boundaries of what is possible, through play. At other times, you will need to feed their natural curiosity, to explain about the world in which they live. This builds confidence as they learn to adapt to a wider variety of situations. Understanding brings freedom.

LEARNING STEP BY STEP

When a baby starts out in life, they learn simple things. Gradually, learning builds on these very early understandings and leads to more complex ideas. For example, a baby may at first be fascinated by their pram rattle, by the noise it makes and the way it bounces when the pram is moved. Later, they may build an appreciation of roundness, of pattern or of colours on to this early fascination. Eventually, they will associate the spoken word, 'rattle', with it, and even the names of colours – 'red', 'white', 'blue', and so on. This is now becoming quite a complex body of knowledge, and the toddler can move around and investigate other items that have roundness, other patterns, and therefore link the nature of the rattle to that of other real-life objects.

In learning, the young child moves from the simple to the complex, from real-life understanding to the use of words or numbers to define what they see, touch, smell, taste and hear. In this learning process, rhymes, riddles and songs can have an invaluable place as long as they represent experiences that the learner is reasonably familiar with. For example, a rhyme about running is not particularly pertinent to a child who is not yet walking well, and a song like 'Lavender's blue' may well mean very little to a child who does not know their colours.

MAKING THE IDEAS IN THE RHYME CLEAR

Learning is also connected with clarity. For example, parents often entertain young toddlers with 'Baa, Baa, Black Sheep', which they find highly enjoyable, particularly if there is a picture to look at or toys to show the action. As time progresses, they recognise 'black', 'the little boy' (who lives down the lane) and 'sheep', but unless you as a parent show them, only later is the word 'wool' understood. For this reason, rhymes and riddles are used ('Jack **fell down**', 'Humpty Dumpty had a great **fall**'). Pictures with little cardboard characters to animate the rhymes make them even more enjoyable and memorable, because your child can see the character falling, running, or eating. On the other hand, a rhyme like 'Round and round the garden', enjoyed by children even in the infant school, is easily acted out using finger play.

RHYMES INCLUDED IN THIS BOOK

Most of the best known rhymes are included in this book, even when some objects or words have gone out of fashion or are remote from a child's experience. Some rhymes are so delightful that to give them a miss just because of a word (which can be easily explained anyway) would be very unfortunate. 'Pease Porridge' may not mean much to a three year old nowadays, but this can be explained, and the second verse will mean much more to your child:

Some like it hot,
Some like it cold,
Some like it in the pot,
Nine days old.

Baby and finger rhymes are included because these are sung and recited at three years, four years, and for some years after.

2 Baby and Toddler Rhymes

These are also called finger rhymes and appeal not only to babies and toddlers, but also to older pre-school children. In fact, finger rhymes can also be used with infants. They include: 'This little piggy', 'Pat-a-cake', 'Round and round the garden', 'Two little dicky birds'. Others have body movements to illustrate the rhyme: 'I'm a little teapot', 'Jelly on a plate'.

FINGER RHYMES

This little piggy (pig) went to
  market,
This little piggy (pig) stayed at
  home,
This little piggy (pig) had roast beef,
This little piggy (pig) had none,
This little piggy (pig) cried,
  'Wee-wee-wee,
All the way home'.

(Touch each toe in turn, starting with the big toe, and on the last line tickle underneath your child's foot.)

Round and round the garden,
Went the teddy bear,
One step,
Two step,
Tickle under there.

(Run your finger round your child's palm. 'One step, two step'
is up his arm. The last line is a tickle under his arm.)

Pat-a-cake, pat-a-cake,
Baker's man,
Bake a cake,
As fast as you can.
Pat it and prick it
And mark it with B,
And put it in the oven,
For Baby and me.

(Claps hands, even perhaps helping your child (Baby) to clap
her hands.)

Two little dicky-birds sitting on a
  wall,
One named Peter, one named Paul.
Fly away Peter, fly away Paul,
Come back Peter, come back Paul.

(Stick two small pieces of paper on to each forefinger for Peter
and Paul. Show to your child and then for 'Fly away...' put the
hands down and change for the index finger. Then bring
'...back Peter' etc.

BODY MOVEMENTS

Jelly on a plate,
Jelly on a plate,
Wibble–wobble,
Wibble–wobble,
Jelly on a plate.

(Your child can wibble–wobble arms, legs and body while
sitting down, or standing up.)
   Other items can be used for 'jelly' – custard, other wobbly
puddings.

I'm a little teapot, short and stout,
Here's my handle, here's my spout.
When I see the teacups, hear me
  shout,
'Tip me up and pour me out'.

(At the second line your child can put one hand on their hip, and the other as a spout.)

LEARNING POINTS

Most of these rhymes are extremely entertaining for small children. In these days of tea bags, though, your child may not know what a teapot is. If they have a tea set, you can lay out the cups, saucers and the teapot, and use them to illustrate the rhyme. You can fill the teapot with water and fill the teacups to show what 'Tip me up and pour me out' means.

3 Early Rhymes for Word Knowledge and Counting

Early rhymes that can extend word knowledge and counting include:

- Incy wincy spider
- Baa, baa black sheep
- Hickory dickory dock
- Hey diddle diddle
- Humpty Dumpty
- Hot cross buns
- All good children count together
- If you're happy and you know it, clap your hands

    stamp your feet

    nod your head

    wave your hand

- It's raining, it's pouring
- One man went to mow
- One finger, one thumb   } The body parts
- Heads and shoulders
- Polly put the kettle on.

These rhymes have simpler words and counting than many other rhymes, and will tend to build on what your child knows at about three years of age. Don't forget, though, that children love the rhymes when they are older, so sing and recite them to older children too.

Incy, wincy spider,
Climbing up the spout,
Down came the rain
And washed the spider out.
Out came the sun
Dried up all the rain
Incy, wincy spider
Climbing up again.

Using a cut-out spider, you can show how the spider first runs
up, falls **down**, then climbs **up** again.

Baa, baa black sheep
Have you any wool?
Yes sir, yes sir,
Three bags full.
One for the master,
One for the dame,
One for the little boy,
Who lives down the lane.

This is a very simple counting rhyme and you can use your
fingers to show the number of bags.

Hickory dickory dock
The mouse ran up the clock
The clock struck one
The mouse ran down
Hickory dickory dock.

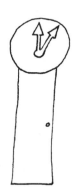

As with Incy wincy spider, you can use a cut-out clock (or toy clock) and run a cut-out cardboard mouse up and down it.

Humpty Dumpty sat on a wall
Humpty Dumpty had a great fall
All the king's horses and all the
  king's men
Couldn't put Humpty together again.

Like all rhymes, Humpty Dumpty is something to talk about with your child 'Isn't it sad...?' But also emphasise falling **down** and the danger of certain situations.

Hey diddle diddle,
The cat and the fiddle,
The cow jumped over the moon.
The little dog laughed to see such
   fun,
And the dish ran away with the
   spoon.

This is a nonsense rhyme of five short lines with many
interesting characters to talk about – cat, fiddle, cow, moon,
dog, dish, spoon. There are also action words – jumped over,
laughed, ran away.

Hot cross buns,
Hot cross buns,
One a penny,
Two a penny,
Hot cross buns!

(Option for)

If you have no daughters
Give them to your sons
One a penny, two a penny
Hot cross buns.

This rhyme has relatively simple words and is useful for early reading. Also, there is the beginning of counting so you can use fingers (or objects).

If you're happy and you know it clap
  your hands.
If you're happy and you know it clap
  your hands.
If you're happy and you know it and
  you really want to show it,
If you're happy and you know it clap
  your hands.

2nd   stamp your feet
3rd   nod your head
4th   wave your hand

Although there are many actions in this rhyme, they are easy to learn and are suitable for a very young child. The repetition helps memorisation but overall the song is about being **happy**.

One man went to mow,
Went to mow a meadow,
One man and his dog, Woof! Woof!
Went to mow a meadow.

Two men went to mow,
Went to mow a meadow,
Two men, one man and his dog,
  Woof! Woof!
Went to mow a meadow. Etc.

This is a useful counting rhyme, but at first it is best to limit it to two or three verses, or take guidance from your child's interest and enjoyment. Sing it fairly slowly, particularly at first. Using cardboard cut-outs of men and a dog makes it very enjoyable, too.

Polly put the kettle on
Polly put the kettle on
Polly put the kettle on
We'll all have tea.

Sukey take it off again
Sukey take it off again
Sukey take it off again
They've all gone away.

This teaches opposites (on/off) and tells a story – someone comes, they have tea, they go away. Using dolls and a tea set can enliven this very popular game.

It's raining, it's pouring,
The old man is snoring,
He went to bed
And bumped his head,
And couldn't get up in the morning.

The rhyme and rhythm in this are both very memorable – you could call this a 'catchy' nursery rhyme.

One finger, one thumb, keep moving,
One finger, one thumb, keep moving,
One finger, one thumb, keep moving,
We'll all be merry and bright.

2nd One finger, one thumb, one arm,
      keeping moving,
3rd One finger, one thumb, one arm,
      one leg, keep moving,
4th One finger, one thumb, one arm,
      one leg, one nod of the head.

Each part of the body is indicated as mentioned. This rhyme covers quite a few body parts and is very much enjoyed, particularly by a group of children.

Heads and shoulders, knees and
  toes, knees and toes
Heads and shoulders, knees and
  toes, knees and toes
Heads and shoulders, knees and
  toes,

Heads and shoulders, knees and
  toes, knees and toes.

As with the previous rhyme, the body part can be indicated as
it is sung.

All good (God's) children count
  together,
One, two, three, four, five,
All good children count together,
One, two, three, four, five,
One, two, three, four, five,
We're glad we are alive.
All good children count together,
One, two, three, four, five.

Ken Adams

2nd 'Clap together'
3rd 'Stamp together'. Etc.

You can line up your child's dolls/teddies and count them with the song, or count along his or her fingers.

The music for 'All good children' is written below.

4 More Involved Rhymes for Your Child

The words, sentences and ideas represented in the following rhymes are, in general, more complex than in the previous chapter, and therefore are more suitable for a slightly older pre-school child. However, some of these rhymes are popular at a younger age, so no hard and fast line has been drawn as to when a child should be introduced to which rhyme. It is up to you as a parent to try to assess what your child can reasonably easily understand in a rhyme and which rhyme is far too complex and will spoil enjoyment.

Jack and Jill went up the hill
To fetch a pail of water.
Jack fell down
And broke his crown
And Jill came tumbling after.

This is a reasonably simple rhyme that teaches up/down, fetch, broke, tumbling, fell.

Sally go round the sun,
Sally go round the moon,
Sally go round the chimney pots,
On a Sunday afternoon.

Again, this is a fairly simple rhyme apart from the reference to chimney pots, which may need explaining. You can get your child to illustrate 'round' by sweeping your finger in a horizontal circle with 'go round'. Your child will learn more if the days of the week are substituted for 'Sunday' for the following verses. Don't be too rigorous, though – the emphasis needs to be on enjoyment.

Twinkle, twinkle, little star,
How I wonder what you are.
Up above the sky so high,
Like a diamond in the sky.
Twinkle, twinkle, little star,
How I wonder what you are.

You may need to explain what a diamond is. If possible, get your child to stick adhesive stars on a sheet of paper. Even more interesting for your child is to show them what 'twinkle' means by looking at stars in the sky on a clear night. This can be a fascinating and memorable experience for a young child.

One potato, two potato
Three potato, four,
Five potato, six potato
Seven potato more.

This is a good counting rhyme. Get your child to clench both fists and build imaginary towers in the air with each new number.

A sailor went to sea, sea, sea,
To see what he could see, see, see.
But all that he could see, see, see,
Was the bottom of the deep blue
   sea, sea, sea.

For very young children this rhyme can be confusing because of the familiar sounding 'see' and 'sea', but for an older child the use of 'sea' and 'see' in repetition is fascinating. If your child is ready, point out the different spelling between 'sea' and 'see', and their different meanings.

This old man, he played one,
He played nick-nack on my drum,
With a nick-nack paddy whack,
Give a dog a bone,
This old man came rolling home.

2nd This old man, he played two,
          ...... shoe

3rd	played three,
	. . . . . . knee
4th	played four,
	. . . . . . door
5th	played five,
	. . . . . . hive
6th	played six,
	. . . . . . sticks

Take your lead from your child for this counting rhyme. To increase interest, line up counters/marbles/pencils/crayons for real-life counting.

Row, row, row your boat,
Gently down the stream;
Merrily, merrily, merrily, merrily,
Life is but a dream.

Sit on the floor opposite your child, hold hands and rock backwards and forwards to simulate rowing. You can add for line 2 'Gently to the sea' and for line 4 'Be home in time for tea'. Using a little toy rowing boat with oars, and a toy man inside, can illustrate this rhyme well.

The bear walked over the mountain,
The bear walked over the mountain,
The bear walked over the mountain,
To see what he could see.

But all that he could see,
But all that he could see,
Was the other side of the mountain,
The other side of the mountain,
The other side of the mountain,
Was all that he could see.

Send your child walking round the room for this one. For
further verses there can be other actions to perform: ran,
hopped, jumped, crawled etc.

Old MacDonald had a farm,
E-I-E-I-O!
And on that farm he had some cows,
E-I-E-I-O!
With a moo-moo, here, a moo-moo
   there,

Here a moo, there a moo,
Everywhere a moo-moo!
Old MacDonald had a farm,
E-I-E-I-O!

For further verses you can replace cow/moo with duck/quack, dog/woof, cat/miaow etc. This links well with any farm set that your child has amongst their toys.

To extend the play and learning, you can change the farm to a zoo, a house, or a fair to extend to other animals and noises, or simply to show someone (e.g. Mum/Dad) or something (big wheel) by actions.

Here we go round the Mulberry
  bush,
The Mulberry bush, the Mulberry
  bush,
Here we go round the Mulberry
  bush,
On a cold and frosty morning.

Hold hands with your child and dance round.

Other verses to add are:

2nd This is the way we wash our
    clothes.
3rd This is the way we eat our food.
4th This is the way we drink our
    drink.
5th This is the way we climb the
    stairs. Etc.

This teaches and emphasises many actions and sounds (witness
your child's very realistic slurping of an imaginary drink).

The wheels on the bus go round and
    round, round and round, round and
    round:
The wheels on the bus go round and
    round,
All day long.

2nd The horn on the bus goes
     Beep! Beep! Beep!
3rd The driver of the bus says 'Any
     more fares?'
4th The Mummies on the bus go,
     'Chatter, chatter, chatter!'
5th The babies on the bus go
     'Waaa, waaa, waaa!'
6th The doggies on the bus go
     'Woof! Woof! Woof!'
7th The Grandmas on the bus say
     'Mind my toes, dear!'. Etc.

Inside, outside, upside down,
Round about, and up the town.
Clap your hands and stamp your
  feet,
Squirm about upon the seat.

                              Ken Adams

Use the actions mentioned for this rhyme.

The music for 'Inside, Outside' is written below.

5 Slightly More Complex Rhymes and Some Story Rhymes

Story rhymes of a simple kind include:

- Ding, dong bell
- Little Bo-Peep
- Georgie Porgie
- Little Miss Muffit
- Oh, the grand old Duke of York
- Pussy cat, pussy cat
- Hush-a-bye baby
- Ladybird, ladybird.

Ding, dong bell,
Pussy's in the well,
Who put him in?
Little Johnny Green.
Who pulled him out?
Little Tommy Stout.
What a naughty boy was that,
To try to drown poor pussy cat.

This is a good vehicle for acting between a couple of friends of siblings. A toy cat should be used.

Ladybird, ladybird, fly away home;
Your house is on fire, and your
   children all gone;
All but the youngest, whose name is
   Anne,
And she hid under the frying pan.

Like the following rhyme, this tells a simple (but sad) story as
dramatic as a modern TV soap. It helps to link to story reading
as your child begins to read. Such rhymes are also a good
basis for helping those who can read a little but need to
expand their word knowledge.

Pussy cat, pussy cat,
Where have you been?
I've been to London
To look at the Queen.
Pussy cat, pussy cat,
What did you there?
I frightened a little mouse
Under her chair.

Little Miss Muffit
Sat on a tuffet
Eating her curds and whey
Along came a spider,
Who sat down beside her,
And frightened Miss Muffit away.

You can explain away 'tuffet' as a seat and 'curds and whey' as dinner. Use your hand and fingers as a 'spider' if you wish, to demonstrate the action to your child.

Oh, the grand old Duke of York,
He had ten thousand men,
He marched them up to the top of
  the hill,
And marched them down again.
And when they were up, they were up,
And when they were down, they
  were down,
And when they were only half way
  up,
They were neither up nor down.

This has to be explained in terms of a general who took his army to the top of the hill, and marched them down again. 'Half way' can be shown as not up, not down, but somewhere in the middle. It works with this age group because it is a very tuneful rhyme, and most of the words are simple, emphasising a simple up/down idea.

Georgie Porgie, pudding and pie,
Kissed the girls and made them cry.
When the boys came out to play,
Georgie Porgie ran away.

This neat, carefully sounded rhyme teaches rhythm and rhyme well. The words are simplistic, and help with reading.

Hush-a-bye baby,
In the tree top.
When the wind blows,
The cradle will rock.
When the bow breaks,
The cradle will fall,
And down will come baby,
Cradle and all.

This a gentle rhyme, perhaps to sing quietly at bedtime, and can be used as a lullaby from a very early age. Later, it can be seen as a story rhyme (watch out for some very prying questions about what the baby is up there for, in the first place!).

Little Bo-Peep
Has lost her sheep,
And doesn't know where to find
  them.
Leave them alone,
And they will come home,
Dragging their tails behind them.

Other rhymes given below show some story form, but may have difficult words or ideas in them.

There was a little girl,
Who had a little curl,
Right in the middle of her forehead.
When she was good,
She was very, very good,
And when she was bad,
She was horrid.

'Curl', and 'forehead' and 'horrid' need to be explained sometimes. Girls, in particular, will often identify with this rhyme, and, even at this young age, recognise the inference to their nice/naughty nature.

Half a pound of tuppenny rice,
Half a pound of treacle,
That's the way the money goes –
Pop, goes the weasel!

This is a very rhythmic and memorable rhyme. It teaches relatively little, apart from rhythm but is certainly remembered well!

London Bridge is falling down,
Falling down, falling down,
London Bridge is falling down,
My fair lady.

This rhyme can be illustrated by hand movements to show 'falling down'. The rhyme is memorable for its fine tune.

1, 2, 3, 4, 5
Once I caught a fish alive.
6, 7, 8, 9, 10
Then I let it go again.

Why did you let it go?
Because it bit my finger so
Which finger did it bite?
This little finger on my right.

This is both a counting **and** a story rhyme. The wording is fairly simple, so this can be used to strengthen word knowledge and early reading skills. The numbers can be written as 1, 2... etc, or as one, two... etc. (which also helps spelling for a better reader).

Pease porridge hot,
Pease porridge cold,
Pease porridge in the pot,
Nine days old.

Some like it hot,
Some like it cold,
Some like it in the pot,
Nine days old.

Another opposite occurs here – hot/cold – and the rhyme suggests the variety of people's tastes. Ask your child 'Would you like porridge left in the pot for nine days?'

See-saw Margery Daw,
Jacky shall have a new master;
He shall have but a penny a day,
Because he can't work any faster!

This is a gentle, rocking rhyme that is often sung at a younger age. There are simple words which strengthen word knowledge, even when the **overall** meaning is not clear.

Girls and boys come out to play,
The moon doth shine as bright as
    day.
Leave your supper and leave your
    sleep,
Come with your play fellows in the
    street.
Come with a whoop, and come with
    a call,
Come with a good will, or not at all.

This rhyme is a happy, dancing one and the rather simple wording is helpful to early reading and spelling.

Ring-a-ring-o-roses,
A pocket full of posies,
Atishoo, atishoo,
We all fall down.

Although this is a poem about the Great Plague in the seventeenth century, to a pre-school child it is a rhyme to join hands with Mummy and dance around to fall down on the last line. In other words, it is a bit of fun, and no explanations are necessarily needed.

Now follow three little rhymes.

Little Boy Blue,
Come blow your horn,
The sheep's in the meadow,
The cow's in the corn.

Where is the little boy,
Who looks after the sheep?
He's under the haystack,
Fast asleep!

Will you wake him?
No, not I!
For if I do,
He's sure to cry.

This is story form, the words are simple, and aid early reading.
You will probably have to explain about meadow and haystack,
though.

Mary had a little lamb,
It's fleece was white as snow,
And everywhere that Mary went,
The lamb was sure to go.

'Fleece' will need to be explained, and many children are
ignorant of 'lamb', since most do not live in the country. 'As
white as snow' is an excellent expression to learn at a young
age (hopefully, your child has seen snow!)

Little Jack Horner,
Sat in a corner,
Eating his Christmas Pie,
He put in a thumb,
Pulled out a plum,

And said, 'What a good boy am I!'

You can illustrate this rhyme to your child by actions, using hands and fingers and a plastic mixing bowl. The humour is very strong throughout and is liked for that reason.

6 Complex Rhymes and Story Rhymes

These are suitable for the older pre-school child, or early school learner.

In this section are many rhymes which are carried forward by children for several years. Nine year olds and older still use 'Miss Polly had a dolly' in ball and skipping games. They will teach reading, counting, spelling, rhythm and rhyming to your child. For very capable children, many of these rhymes can be learnt at an earlier age, but some definitely need that touch of 'maturity' to interest a child. Some are rhymes, some are songs, and some are simply short stories in rhyme form. They all form an invaluable aid to the learning of basic skills for your child.

Jack Sprat could eat no fat,
His wife could eat no lean,
So between the two of them,
They licked the platter clean.

Children find this surprisingly difficult, possibly because of words like 'lean' and 'platter', and the **idea** needs to be explained carefully.

Goosey, goosey, gander,
Where shall I wander?

Upstairs, downstairs,
In my lady's chamber.
There I met an old man
Who wouldn't say his prayers,
I took him by the left leg
And threw him down the stairs.

Wee Willie Winkie,
Runs through the town,
Upstairs and downstairs,
In his nightgown.
Rapping at the window,
Crying through the lock,
'Are the children in their beds,
It's past eight o'clock?'

These are 'straight' rhymes without a tune, but have the advantage of much action, some of it extraordinary. ('Why did he throw that old man down the stairs?', said John, aged three. 'It's just a silly rhyme', I said).

There are several more complex number rhymes that can be learnt at this slightly older age.

One, two, buckle my shoe;
Three, four, knock at the door;
Five, six, pick up sticks;
Seven, eight, lay them straight;
Nine, tine, my fat hen;
Eleven, twelve, dig and delve;
Thirteen, fourteen, maids a-courting;
Fifteen, sixteen, maids in the
     kitchen;
Seventeen, eighteen, maids in
     waiting;
Nineteen, twenty, my plate's empty.

Other rhymes start at a number and work back. Choose where your child starts (at 5 or 10, for example, or even at 3).

There were ten in the bed,
And the little one said,
'Roll over! Roll over!'
So they all rolled over
And one fell out.
There were nine in the bed . . . etc.

Ten green bottles,
Hanging on the wall,
Ten green bottles,
Hanging on the wall,
And if one green bottle
Should accidentally fall,
There'd be nine green bottles
Hanging on the wall.
Nine green bottles... etc.

The first line can be changed to ten big soldiers, or ten big teddies, or ten little monkeys. Use fingers as you count out, but bear in mind that this is a **subtraction** exercise, so can be difficult for some.

There was an old man called Michael
   Finnigin,
He grew whiskers on his chin-igin,
The wind came out and blew them
   in-igin,
Poor old Michael Finnigin...
Begin-igin!

This is a clapping song to enjoy rhythm and rhyme.

Orange and lemons,
Say the bells of St Clement's.
You owe me five farthings,
Say the bells of St Martin's.
When will you pay me?
Say the bells of Old Bailey.
When I grow rich,
Say the bells of Shoreditch.
When will that be?
Say the bells of Stepney.
I'm sure I don't know,
Say the great bells of Bow.
Here comes a candle to light you to
  bed,
Here comes a chopper to chop off his
  head!

The last two lines are a game between several children. Two
hold hands, and the others pass beneath, hoping to miss the
'chopper'.

Miss Polly had a dolly who was sick,
sick, sick.
So she called for the doctor to be
quick, quick, quick.
The doctor came with his bag and
his hat,
And he knocked at the door with a
rat-a-tat-tat.
He looked at Dolly, and he shook his
head,
And he said, 'Miss Polly, put her
straight to bed'.
He wrote on a paper for a pill, pill,
pill,
'That will make her better, yes it
will, will, will'.

This is a story rhyme much beloved by girls (and boys) of ages
from four or five years up to ten or eleven. It is a skipping and
bouncing a ball on the wall game. It has good rhythm and
rhyme, and an enjoyable tune.

Dance to your daddy,
My little laddie,
Dance to your daddy,
My little lamb!
You shall have a fishy
On a little dishy,
You shall have a fishy
When the boat comes in.

This beautiful song tells of fisherman. It will help if you explain
to your child what the lines mean.

Lavender's blue, dilly, dilly,
Lavender's green;
When I am king, dilly, dilly,
You shall be queen.

Skip, skip, skip to my lou,
Skip, skip, skip to my lou,
Skip, skip, skip to my lou,
Skip to my lou, my darling.

Skip round on the spot with your child.

Bobby Shafto's gone to sea,
Silver buckles on his knee,
He'll come back and marry me,
Bonny Bobby Shafto!

These three rhymes have fairly simple wording and good tunes
to improve word knowledge and basic spelling.

Here we go looby lou,
Here we go looby light,
Here we go looby lou,
All on a Saturday night.

You put your right foot in,
You put your right foot out,
In, out, in, out,
Shake it all about.
You do the hokey-cokey
Then you turn around,
That's what it's all about.
Oh, hokey, cokey, cokey,
Oh, hokey, cokey, cokey,

Oh, hokey, cokey, cokey,
In, out, in, out, ra, ra, ra.

The Hokey Cokey teaches many actions, left/right, in/out, and is an aid to memorisation. When it is learnt it is extremely enjoyable for your child. Take it easy at first because your child may find it complex. Later add:

You put your left foot in, etc.
                  right hand in...
                  left hand in...
                  whole self in...

She'll be coming round the mountain
        when she comes, toot, toot!
She'll be coming round the mountain
        when she comes, toot, toot!
She'll be coming round the mountain
        – coming round the mountain,
She'll be coming round the mountain
        when she comes, toot, toot!

2nd She'll be riding six white horses
       when she comes, whoah back, etc.
3rd We'll all go out to meet her
       when she comes, Hi Babe, etc.
4th And we'll kill the old red rooster
       when she comes, chop, chop!
       Etc.

This is an action rhyme and also for making noises. Your child
can act out 'coming round', 'riding', 'meet her' (waving),
'chop, chop' (using a hand).

Yankee Doodle went to town,
Riding on a pony;
He stuck a feather in his cap,
And called it macaroni.

Although the following is a lullaby, most children (and many
teenagers and adults) are fascinated by the twists and turns of
this rhyme:

Hush little baby, don't say a word,
Papa's going to buy you a mocking
    bird.

If that mocking bird won't sing,
Papa's going to buy you a diamond
   ring.
If that diamond ring turns brass,
Papa's going to buy you a looking
   glass.
If that looking glass gets broke,
Papa's going to buy you a billy goat.
If that billy goat won't pull,
Papa's going to buy you a cart and
   bull.
If that cart and bull turn over,
Papa's going to buy you a dog
   named Rover.
If that dog named Rover won't bark,
Papa's going to buy you a horse and
   cart.
If that horse and cart fall down,
You'll still be the sweetest little baby
   in town.

7 A Few Longer Rhymes, and some with Deeper Meanings

In a dark, dark wood, there's a
   dark, dark house,
In a dark, dark house, there's a
   dark, dark room,
In a dark, dark room, there's a dark,
   dark cupboard
In a dark, dark cupboard, there's a
   dark, dark box,
In the dark, dark box, there's a
   (ghost, monster, etc).

The first rhyme 'In a dark, dark wood' has mystery and
excitement. At the end you can ask your child to say what is in
the box. In the following tongue-twister, let your child try to
say *each line* after you.

Peter Piper picked a peck of pickled
   pepper;
A peck of pickled pepper Peter Piper
   picked;

If Peter Piper picked a peck of
  pickled pepper,
Where's the peck of pickled pepper
  Peter Piper picked?

'Soloman Grundy' helps to teach the days of the week; but it
also wraps up a whole life and is a 'moral' to a child.

Solomon Grundy, born on Monday,
Christened on Tuesday,
Married on Wednesday,
Took ill on Thursday,
Worse on Friday,
Died on Saturday,
Buried on Sunday,
That was the end
Of Solomon Grundy.

Old King Cole,
Was a merry old soul,
And a merry old soul was he;
He called for his pipe,

And he called for his bowl,
And he called for his fiddlers three.

There was a crooked man,
And he walked a crooked mile,
He found a crooked sixpence,
Against a crooked stile:
He bought a crooked cat,
Which caught a crooked mouse,
And they all lived together,
In a little crooked house.

This rhyme is notable for the repetition of 'crooked' and how
it fits into the sense of the whole rhyme. 'There was an old
woman' is a famous old rhyme that, quite simply, fascinates.

There was an old woman who lived
  in a shoe,
She had so many children,
She didn't know what to do.
She gave them some broth without
  any bread,

And scolded them soundly,
And sent them to bed.

The farmer's in his den,
The farmer's in this den,
E...I...E...I,
The farmer's in his den.

2nd The farmer picks a wife...
3rd The wife picks a child...
4th The child picks a nurse...
5th The nurse picks a dog...
6th We all pat the dog...

One child in a group stands in the middle. He or she chooses a wife, the wife chooses a child, etc. Your child can play this with dolls and you.

'Three blind mice' has a very notable tune.

Three blind mice,
See how they run!
They all ran off with the farmer's
    wife,

Who cut off their tails with a
    carving knife,
Did you ever see such a thing in
    your life,
As three blind mice.

Old Mother Hubbard,
Went to the cupboard,
To fetch the poor doggy a bone.
But when she got there,
The cupboard was bare,
And so the poor dog had none.
She went to the baker's,
To buy him some bread;
But when she came back,
The poor dog was dead.
She took a clean dish,
To get him some tripe;
But when she came back,
He was smoking a pipe.
She went to the tailor's

To buy him a coat;
But when she came back,
He was riding a goat.
She went to the hatter's,
To buy him a hat;
But when she came back,
He was feeding the cat.
She went to the cobbler's
To buy him some shoes;
But when she came back,
He was reading the news.
The dame made a curtsy,
The dog made a bow;
The dame said, 'Your servant',
The dog said 'Bow-wow'.

These larger and more involved rhymes tell stories in fairly simple language, and are valuable to teach reading, spelling, rhythm, pitch, rhyme and word knowledge. They also add great enjoyment to your child's knowledge and understanding of the world.

8 Using Riddles

Rhymes and songs provide a pre-school child with a 'bank' of spoken words, of some recognised reading words, and interest in counting and numbers. They also give a life-long love of rhythm and rhyme. Riddles, on the other hand, will stimulate your child to think, and, perhaps more importantly, will help them to *enjoy* thinking.

For this age group there must be a clear link in the mind with what is heard. The riddle, in other words, must evoke an image fairly easily. Difficult or old fashioned words must be eliminated. The easiest way to stimulate thinking, and yet still retain interest is to provide an object, or the picture of an object, and ask what it is.

I am long and wriggle.
What am I?

The clue needs to be *read* to your child.

I roar and live in the jungle.
What am I?

I cut things.
What am I?

This type of riddle is fairly easy for most pre-school children. The objects are from real-life, from their experience, and they are 'concrete'.

What is more difficult is to introduce more abstract words

and ideas. The simplest type of riddle to test and stretch pre-school thinking is the following (in these, you ask the questions):

What is cold? The answer could be an ice-cream or snow.

What is hot?

What is small?

What is soft?

What is yellow?

What is round?

More difficult words are involved in:

What is rough?

What is smooth?

What is day?

What is night?

What is round?

What is square?

For those who need more stimulation, a combination of words and ideas is necessary:
I am nearly round, I am quite small and I have prickles all over me. (Answer hedgehog.)

To make the 'game' more interesting, it helps to start with 'riddle-me-ree'.

Riddle-me-ree, look at me.
I am yellow. I am quite long.
People peel me and eat me.
What am I? (Answer banana.)

Be patient with your child, though, in riddle solving. They do stretch thinking, but a child can be 'put off' quite easily if the success rate is not high.